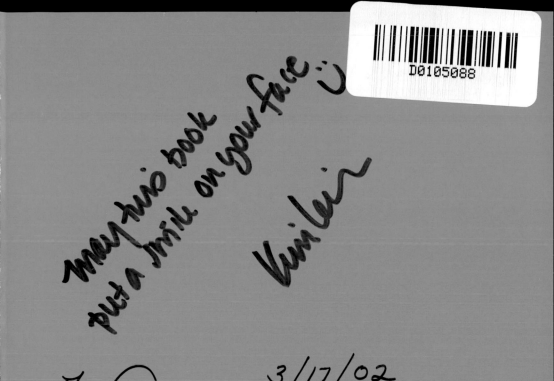

may this book
put a smile on your face :)

Kimberlin

3/17/02

To Pam,
   In memory of Mya.
Love,
   Pat & Paul

Erin Go Bark!

Irish Dogs and Blessings

A Bark & Smile™ Book

Photographed by Kim Levin
Written by John O'Neill

**Andrews McMeel
Publishing**
Kansas City

To our dads, whose love of the Irish
(and dogs) inspired this book

01 02 03 04 05 TWP 10 9 8 7 6 5 4 3 2 1

ISBN 0-7407-1461-9

Library of Congress Catalog Card Number: 00-106944

Book design by Holly Camerlinck

www.barkandsmile.com

Preface

🍀

It seems fitting to share the history behind *Erin Go Bark! Irish Dogs and Blessings.* We went to Ireland in March 1999. It was a great opportunity to photograph the dogs there and have a few pints of Guinness along the way! We were shocked by how many dogs we saw roaming the streets and country-side. They had a lot of character, just like the dogs in the United States. They were scruffy, wet, and quite independent— many have never seen a leash or collar—but also very loyal and protective.

For twelve days we drove from Dublin to Kinsale to Dingle Bay to Galway, photographing every dog we encountered along the way. We had the time of our lives, and we even got engaged during the trip. This book is dear to both of us because it will always be a visual reminder of a very special time in our lives.

Thanks to all the Irish dogs and their owners who let us experience Ireland in such a special way. Thank you to Rick for all his time and effort. Thanks to our parents for their love and support. Finally, thank you to Patty Rice at Andrews McMeel Publishing who saw the humor and sentimentality in *Erin Go Bark!*

Erin Go Bark!

May you welcome
the ones you love
and even the ones
you don't.

May your lazy afternoons
stay that way.

Erin Go Bark!

May you always eavesdrop
on good news.

6

May you seek revenge
on the person
who named you "Scruffy."

May you see the
inside of the door
as often as you see
the outside.

May Mother Nature always
give you the best baths.

As you perch yourself
on the same old stairs,
may yesterday's woes
be today's love affairs.

May a doggy bag
always reward your wait.

May getting down
be easier than getting up.

May the person
who brushes your hair
have a gentle hand.

May your paws never slip . . .

... *when you stretch.*

May the sun keep you warm,
and the ground keep you cool.

May the feeling of a warm hug
come at least once a day.

May your walks never end
before you want them to.

May the next person
who calls you "Lassie"
get fleas.

May you never have
a "nine to five."

May you put a smile on the face
of the next one you meet.

May your legs always remain
as strong as your will to run.

When you're feeling lonely,
may your tail still wag, and . . .

. . . may a new friend
be just around the corner.

Erin Go Bark!

May your local open early
and close late.

May your owner
never play off-key.

Let us forever bless
the witty soul
who invented dog clothing.

May the smile on your face
get bigger every day.

May you always find the time
for family outings.

May you leave
a lasting impression
on those who pass you by.

May your bed stay warm,
your bowl stay full,
and may you live
a long and healthy life.

May you always
catch your breath
at the top of the hill.

In all that you do,
may you always find
a helping hand.

Be curious,
like an Irish rover . . .

. . . and mysterious,
like a four-leaf clover.

May your coat stay shiny,
your nose stay cold,
and the sidewalk stay soft.

May you never have to worry about covering your mouth when you yawn.

When times get cold and wet,
may your dreams
stay warm and dry.

May you always find happiness
on the road less traveled.

May your friends
always sing your praises
behind your back.

May your ears
never look like this.

The world is your fire hydrant;
unleash your potential!

May you never get stuck
at the end of the queue.

May you never get bored
just shooting the breeze.

May you always understand
what's being said to you.

May the "big dogs" be careful
whom they mess with.

May the mailman
never keep you waiting.

Erin Go Bark!